The Day of My First Driving Lesson

Tiel Aisha Ansari

First Place Winner of The Poetry Box Chapbook Prize 2020

Editing & Book Design: Shawn Aveningo Sanders
Cover Design: Robert R. Sanders
Author photo: Todd Ellner

ISBN: 978-1-948461-71-9
Printed in the United States of America.
Wholesale Distribution via Ingram.

Published by The Poetry Box®, 2021
Portland, Oregon
ThePoetryBox.com

~ In Loving Memory ~

James Spurgeon Jackson, Jr.
1938 - 2018

Maria May Jackson
1941 - 2019

1960

The day my parents went to get the wedding license
the registrar told them the law required a blood test.

The reason was syphilis, but no-one ever said so.
My father's friend Ralph was the son of a doctor.

He opened his office for them although it was a Saturday.
Ralph was a witness at the wedding

and later he married a girl who wasn't Jewish.
His father never spoke to him again. My mother's parents

didn't approve of my dad. But they came to the wedding
and signed the guestbook, their names in Chinese.

In the photo, my parents look impossibly young.
On the license, my father's side says *Colored*.
My mother's side says *Yellow*.

2018

The day I found a cowrie in the sand at Gearhart
cold rain was sweeping in from the ocean.

The cowrie was flawless, porcelain-glossy,
brown with white spots above

delicate teeth washed with pink underneath.
Cowries are native to the tropics.

We used to find them on the beaches of Tanzania
father, mother, brother and me, combing the tidelines.

The sand was hot underfoot
velvet-soft and blindingly white.

The water was warm as a bath.
Salt stung my eyes and burned my throat.

My dad raked over piles of seaweed and picked out shells,
turned them in his long brown fingers.

He showed me cone shells' checkered flanks,
delicate shades of pink and orange inside a conch.

Touched a little octopus in a tidepool—
"Go ahead. No, no, it's not slimy."

Sometimes we'd find the jointed limbs of hermit crabs unfolding
inside our gathered treasures. Then we had to put them back.

Sometimes we didn't find them until we got home
hours later and miles from the ocean.

We put them in water to try to keep them alive
but they died, and I cried.

On a January day at Gearhart
I peered into an implausibly perfect cowrie

checking for slender jointed legs
or for a glimpse of long brown fingers.
Salt water burned my eyes.

2018

The day my father went into hospice care
I took the Orange Line to Milwaukie.

My mother said we shouldn't come to Hawai'i,
it would change nothing, just cause her a lot of stress.

He'd been gone ever since the stroke.
It was more than three years.

I went on with life as if nothing had changed or was about to.
I had planned to go to the Stafford reading: I didn't back out.

It was January. It was fifty-eight degrees.
The sun slanted low and warm across the tracks.
The train rocked me as gently as if it knew.

2018

The day my father died, he told my mother
"I've filled the tank."

In Philadelphia, we owned a blue VW minibus
that my parents drove on family visits

and summer-long cross-country camping trips.
My brother taught me to read in the back seat

from comic books, the summer I was three
according to my parents. I don't remember.

In Tanzania, we owned a white Peugeot 404.
That car was chased by elephants and Cape buffalo

and stopped cold by lions, asleep in the road,
unafraid of the car (slightly annoyed by the horn).

In Hawai'i, we had a bronze Mazda station wagon
formerly owned by Avis. I drove it for my first license test.

My parents bought a camper-pickup and kept it in Las Vegas.
Every year they flew back to the mainland

and drove coast to coast to visit family and friends.
Every year they tried to take a different route.

Blue highways. State and county parks.
KOA or Forest Service campgrounds

until he had his stroke.
The last thing my father said was
"I've crossed the country."

1968

The day John and Tommie raised black-gloved fists
over Olympic gold and under the stars and stripes

I was four years old. Maybe my parents saw the salute.
They would've watched the sprint. Da was track & field in college.

In high school he played hoops. When I was six
we had a Philadelphia '76ers basketball, red, white, and blue.

It was miniature, a toy for kids. We could palm it,
pretend to be Wilt "the Stilt" Chamberlain

or Lou Alcindor, who later changed his name:
Kareem Abdul-Jabbar, superstar, first Muslim in the NBA.

Da coached basketball at every school he worked at in Tanzania
on ragged asphalt red as dirt, hoops rusted, bent, bare of nets.

The boys used whitewash to draw the sidelines, key, free throw line.
My father brought his own whistle and stopwatch.

My mother mimeographed diagrams of the pitch and plays,
carried them on a green vinyl clipboard. My father ran drills.

Dribble. Bounce pass. Dribble. Chest pass.
Free throw. Free throw. Free throw.

Pass around the key and shoot. I sat in the dry grass
and watched. Pass around the key and shoot.

Then choose up teams and scrimmage. Zone defense. Man to man
(boys I thought were men; tall as men, tall as my father).

Seven AM to four PM, my father stood at green chalkboards
chalk dust between his fingers, in front of these tall boys

folded into children's desks, white cotton shirts, indigo shorts
and taught them biology. Physics. The foundations of science.

They never won a lot of games. They went on to be
doctors, engineers, government ministers,

all the heroes a newborn country needs.
My father was a coach of champions.

Back then, the zone defense was legal in the pros.
The three-point shot wasn't a thing yet.

The college basketball tournament goes by a lot of different names:
March Madness, Sweet Sixteen, Elite Eight, Final Four.

My parents watched it every year together.
I watched it with my mother, the last week of her life.
She never got to see the end of the tournament.

2015

The day my father woke and found himself strange—
found only haze in his hazel eyes

the sun rose smoke-stained to bitter orange.
A storm of wings and beaks darkened the sky

hazing the clarity of his hazel eyes.
A mass confusion, mad swirl of birds

whose wings and beaks occupied the skies.
My hands were empty. I had only words.

In mass confusion, mad swirl of birds
there his brain hovered in helpless haze.

My hands were empty. I offered words
as a thread, perhaps, to lead him out of the maze.

My father's brain has hovered in haze
since the day he fell under the lightning stroke.

What thread could lead him out of this maze?
The East Wind's kiss tasted of smoke.

Since the day of the lightning stroke—
the day that the sun rose stained bitter orange—

the East Wind's kiss has lingered in smoke
foreboding a cruel and lasting change
and my father wakes and finds himself strange.

2016

The day I was hit by a car, the ambulance took me to the hospital.
They gave me a CAT scan, then let me go.

Mild concussion, nothing broken.
Bruise on my thigh the size of a grapefruit.

My husband left a message for my mother.
She called back. "Da wants to talk to you."

It was a year after his stroke. He could not speak.
He howled my name over and over.

My mother took back the phone. "Well, as you can tell,
he's quite upset."

"Tell him I'm OK." It's a lie. I'm walking wounded.
"Tell me he's OK." Another lie. He'll never be okay again.
"Tell him I'll be OK."

1989

The day the Nimitz Freeway collapsed, two hundred people died.
I felt the quake, six point nine.

The campus was built to code, built to survive the Big One.
We stood around outside like you're supposed to,

laughing nervously and worrying about the rest of the state.
News started to come through on the radio.

Candlestick Park was safe. The Bay Bridge was broken.
Downtown Santa Cruz looked like a bomb fell on it.

I sneaked into the dorm to call my mother.
"I'm okay. I won't be able to call for a while.

Emergency services need all the phone lines now."
My da heard the news on his way home,

thought he would have to break it to my ma.
She met him at the door to tell him I'd called.

Weeks went by before we talked again. Weeks of aftershocks.
Weeks of digging out roads and digging for bodies.

Months of rebuilding. Months of giant tents on Pacific Avenue.
Hundreds of people displaced. Millions of dollars promised in aid.

I saved my parents a few days of worry.
Small change in the scheme of things.
Numbers don't tell you everything.

1981

The day we drove into Seligman on old Route 66
me and my parents in a rented car

we pulled into Dawn's Cafe. The young fellow at the counter
grinned at my dad. Maybe the only two black men in all of Arizona

in December of 1981 with snow edging the red rimrock,
California behind us and the Grand Canyon ahead.

He said he was from Chicago. I still saw tropical savannas
every time I closed my eyes to sleep. It took us fifteen minutes

just to list the places we'd lived and why. I was seventeen
with miles yet ahead of me and no idea
that I could ever get tired of the road.

1982

The day I fell off a horse—twice—in a pasture overlooking Kailua Bay
high on the slope of Hualalai, the radio played *Jesse's girl...*

in the open back of Lisa's pickup, with Becky, Cherie, Joelle, Kendra:
their hair streaming in the wind, mine braided tight.

In Hawai'i, the sky is the same color as in Tanzania.
Jacarandas cloak hills with the same violet haze.

I'm seventeen, getting ready for college. I want to be a naturalist
like Rachel Carson. Not a crook like Richard Nixon or Frank Rizzo.

Palomino Sitar canters down the slope,
rises at the sawhorses. Becky on his back

looks like she's flying. I want to cheer.
Gentle Gunsmoke's velvet lips pluck a mango from my palm,

leave a smear of slobber. I wipe it on my gray cords,
smell crushed fruit and horse sweat. The radio plays

Got a fever of a hundred and three...
Crimson and clover, over and over...

McDonald's in Kona smells like McDonald's everywhere:
hot grease. Becky plays with the condiment tube,

swats it with her palm, shoots ketchup on my blue chambray shirt,
already smudged with dirt and horse dung from the fall.

Sitar tried to jump with me on board—I wasn't ready
to fly, Sitar. I hit the ground hard enough to feel queasy.

In Hawai'i I'm the same color as everyone else.
In Tanzania I was different from everyone else.

I kept my hair braided so people wouldn't notice it wasn't like theirs.
I'm not used to being treated like a normal person

by girls with horses and radios that play *Don't stop believing...*
Give me a minute. I'll catch my breath.
I'll get up and fly.

1969

The day I got the best advice of my life was the day
I asked my mother, why do some kids believe in Santa?

I knew where gifts came from. Grandparents sent them.
Aunts and uncles. Family friends. *Real* people.

Christmas meant leaving Philadelphia in the dark,
cold dawn over domes with chemical names

looming above the marshes along the New Jersey Turnpike
among strange stinks that woke me in the back seat.

Across tidal flats with no sea in sight
Manhattan's skyline floated against a smoggy horizon:

grey towers over a tangle of asphalt loops,
rows of brownstones, cliffs of New York granite.

In the shadow of the George Washington Bridge
(which I thought of as an extra grandparent)

we ate roast lamb with macaroni and cheese
with my father's family in Yonkers

or after a visit to the Buddhist temple in the Bronx,
noodle soup, stewed pork hocks, peanut and pressed-tofu salad.

I said we shouldn't leave the tree, in case the glass birds
ate the toy fruit decorations. Grownups called me "imaginative."

We unwrapped presents, thank-you-hugged the givers
played Pounce and Scrabble, went to bed in guest rooms

or fell asleep in homebound cars
clutching new toys and warm with hugs.

I couldn't see what Santa had to do with it. I had to ask.
My mother said: "Some people think lying to children
doesn't count as lying."

1982

The day of my first driving lesson, my mother said
"Think of the wheel as a clock face. Your hands at ten and two."

Which made my destination always high noon
and the choices before me love, duty, fear.

Six at the wheel's bottom, six was behind me
but no-one gave me a six-gun or a six-point star

or a guide to my character. Hero, villain, Quaker bride
or dark-skinned woman of a certain reputation.

I learned that it's no good watching the clock.
No-one will tell you when you're called to be a hero.
You have to be ready whenever that noon train rolls in.

1981

The day our freighter docked in Poland, it was spring.
Solidarity was rising in the people's hearts.

So too was the fear of Soviet tanks
rolling to crush the new rebellion.

The captain told my parents we should not leave the ship.
The second officer said we should come visit Gdansk.

Gdansk was his home, a few miles away on the coast.
Gdansk was the center of the Solidarity movement—

Free Port Danzig, with its centuries of history
resisting one occupation after another behind its walls of stone.

We took the train. We saw the memorial at the shipyard,
the three anchors representing hope. We saw the lion

on the old city wall, looking over his shoulder,
watching for the return of an exiled king whose name

the townspeople still remember.
We walked around Gdansk all evening with the young officer.

Poland fell under martial law that year.
I never found out what happened to our host.
I never knew if my parents were afraid.

1979

The day the elephant came wandering through the camp
I sat reading on the cabin porch, pretending I didn't see it

courting—risk? Thrill? My parent's anxious attention?
Until he put his foot on the porch step

(where later I showed my shocked parents
a footprint of crusted dirt just feet from my chair)

inquisitive trunk raised high above my head.
My nerve broke. I crept into the cabin.

The elephant sauntered off through the camp
right past our window, ears billowing like grey sails.

My parents scolded me gently about wild animals
and the difference between caution and fear.

That evening in the outhouse, I heard tearing grass
and looked out to see a vast absence of stars.

The same old bull, grazing his way through camp
not disturbed by a small human with a kerosene lantern.

Whatever held me on the porch was whispering
Go on. It's perfectly safe

this elephant is used to people
and anyway he knows you're here

who are you kidding, this is safety
this outhouse is way too flimsy to protect you

I kept still. My father brought the car to fetch me.
The elephant wandered off.
I think he wondered what all the fuss was about.

1975

The day I complained that I couldn't find anything to read
my parents didn't point impatiently to the crowded bookshelves

all round the house. They dropped me at the library.
Pied crows called from the football pitch

while I learned how to ask for wishes from a sand-fairy
fled across war-torn Europe with a Jewish family

raised a white deer with a mute Aztec boy
roamed the Australian outback with two Abo teens.

I savored the smell of new paper and old paper,
ink and bookbinding glue.

On their way home, my parents picked me up
and asked if I wanted to check out the book I was reading.

I had finished two already. I ground them to flour.
I made them into adventure bread.
I was learning to be the hero of my own story.

2016

The day of the Pride parade, first one after Orlando
was the first day I wore hijab.

I walked with my co-workers, at one end of the banner.
We all wore white T-shirts. My head was covered in blue.

I was walking on air, grin the size of Portland on my face.
You can still find the photo in the school district's archives.

My mother said the picture worried her a little.
"Just parental jitters."

I imagined writing a country-western song:
"If Ma meant me to be a coward
well she done raised me wrong."

2018

The day Hurricane Lane rolled into Hawai'i
I followed the news obsessively

monitored wind speeds near my mother's house
watched smartphone videos of flooded streams.

Five hours away by plane.
Nothing to do to help.

Weather websites marked Lane's past with lines,
projected cones into the future. Hourly updates.

The storm veered north, away from her.
She emailed she was safe

but the exterminator couldn't come. She was getting ready
to sell the house. She couldn't get an appraisal

without termite treatment, they couldn't put up the tent
under threat of hurricane winds.

Lane drifted off into open ocean. My mother was drifting too.
We spent a lot of emails retracing our history.
There was no website to show her future path.

2019

The day my mother went into hospice care
I noticed the smell. Ketosis.

The nurse visited once a day.
My brother and I took turns with my mother

days and nights. We traded shifts
until he had to go home to Boston.

A body devouring itself for energy
smells yeasty-sweet, not unpleasant.

My mother gave me her phone. I answered texts from friends.
"She's comfortable. She sends her love."

A body burning itself for water generates a lot of heat.
I wiped her face and body with wet cloths.

My husband and I stayed in a condo.
He made me shower every evening before I ate.

It wasn't the diaper. You expect that. You cope.
It was the other smell that got into my head.

I made my husband throw out half a loaf of Hawaiian sweetbread.
I tossed my clothes as far as possible from the bed.
I drove to the laundromat with all the windows rolled down.

1982–2019

The day my parents moved into their new house in Hawai'i
was the day Kilauea began to erupt.

It was spring. The jacarandas were blooming.
All the hills above Kona were draped in violet blossoms.

We drove to Volcano National Park and sat in the drizzle
watching fire-fountains dance in the caldera.

Lava flowed off and on for the next thirty-seven years.
Hot stone poured over the cliffs, ate its way through lush forests,

pushed new black cliffs out into the ocean,
burned homes, buried whole towns under new landscapes.

My dad retired from teaching and volunteered at the Park.
The summer after he died, Kilauea's summit shook and collapsed.

The visitor's center at the Park was abandoned.
My mother sent boxes of keepsakes to my brother and me.

Sulphur steam poured from vents, wrapped the slopes in toxic smoke.
People coughed and cursed, rubbed itching eyes,

drove for miles to find clean air on windward shores.
Flowering trees withered in the acid fog.

Kilauea coughed out her last lava flows in November.
The eruption was officially over.

My mother died in March. Ferns were sprouting from cooled lava.
The last jacarandas produced a few pale leaves.
The whole National Park will have to be rebuilt.

2019

The day my mother died was a Saturday.
I stayed in her house until Thursday

flew home on the red-eye and arrived on Friday
went back to work on Monday.

I was born on a Sunday. I was married on a Saturday.
This year, July 4th is a Thursday.

We've made most of our holidays into movable feasts
so we can observe them on Mondays or Fridays.

My mother's birthday was a Thursday this year.
My father's, a Wednesday. My brother's, Tuesday.

This year my birthday falls on a Friday.
Memorial Day is always a Monday. It's a movable feast.
This year I'm observing it every day.

1971

That day, we drove and drove across savannah
to the end of pavement, the edge of jungle.

Then roads of red dirt up the face of the Great Rift
my father steering round hairpin bends

with no guardrails. Thousands of feet straight down,
the bitter lake, stained pink with vast flocks of flamingos.

Onward through fields of upland wheat
then forest, toward the caldera's rim.

Near twilight, a shadow stalked the road's edge.
It sat on its haunches to watch us pass.

It looked in the window,
into my face. Close enough to touch.

Its coat was yellow as dead, sun-dried grass
rosetted black as densest shade. Eyes steady and gold.

Afterward my father said he was too stunned to think,
to stop, take pictures, anything. My mother said

it would have spoiled the moment anyway.
But she was sorry not to have a photo.

She was the one who posed the family for portraits,
caught candid moments on Kodachrome,

assembled albums, made montages, printed calendars
with sepia photos of our great-great-grandparents.

No regrets, Ma. Da at the wheel, you beside him,
a leopard on the shoulder of a dead volcano:
I see you now, and always.

Praise for
The Day of My First Driving Lesson

"I was learning to be the hero of my own story." This line from the poem "1975" could be the anthem for this powerful chapbook that traces the story of the poet's family, an odyssey ranging from coast to coast in the United States, to Tanzania, and beyond. Alternating plainspoken narrative with vivid imagery, the poems also range through time, building a kaleidoscopic view of this interracial family's life, challenges, inevitable aging, and the strong bonds that hold them together even beyond grief. *The Day of My First Driving Lesson* is a rare love letter to good parents and the legacy of compassion they leave behind.

—Amy Miller, Contest Judge, 2020
and author of *The Trouble with New England Girls*

Tiel Aisha Ansari's *The Day of My First Driving Lesson* reads like a memorable road trip through time, each poem noting a point of interest on the journey. Like the hermit crab in one of Ansari's poems, its "jointed limbs...unfolding," the family portrayed here settles into landscapes and cultures as different from each other as Pennsylvania and Tanzania, Hawaii and Oregon. "It took us fifteen minutes," another poem recalls, "just to list the places we'd lived and why." Ansari's poems depict a life shaped by beloved parents and beloved homes, and fueling this collection is the question of how we navigate the eventual loss of those loves. A powerful exploration of what our families can teach us and what we have to learn ourselves along the way, *The Day of My First Driving Lesson* is a poignant, tender collection.

—Jennifer Richter, author of *No Acute Distress* and *Threshold*

A splendidly-woven blend of eulogy and memoir, Tiel Aisha Ansari's stunning new collection of autobiographical poems, like a photo montage of worldwide family travels —deftly arranged by subject, theme, and intuition, rather than by chronology—is full of so much more than what happened where and when. Dedicated to her parents, who died in 2018 and 2019, these precisely detailed, deceptively simple and carefully nuanced poems let us see for ourselves, page by page, memory by memory, the emergence of the poet's personal sense of destiny, as it was shaped within the context of family values and the freedoms they offered. Aware that the choices before her are "love, duty, [and] fear," the poet— like the sheriff in old-time westerns—knows she has "to be ready whenever that noon train rolls in." Readers, prepare yourselves to be swept off your feet by the brilliance and depth of love in this book, by the beauty and power of its understandings. I can't begin to praise it highly enough.

—Ingrid Wendt, author of Evensong

About the Author

 **Tiel Aisha Ansari** is a Sufi warrior poet. She works as a data analyst and professional curmudgeon for the Portland Public School District and is President Emerita of the Oregon Poetry Association. She now hosts the Wider Window Poetry show, promoting the work of poets of color on KBOO Community Radio, (https://www.kboo.fm/program/wider-window-poetry)

Her work has been featured by *Fault Lines Poetry*, *Windfall*, KBOO, and an Everyman's Library anthology, among others. Her collections include *Knocking from Inside*, *High-Voltage Lines*, *Country Well-Known as an Old Nightmare's Stable*, and *Dervish Lions* (forthcoming from Fernwood Press). She drinks coffee in the morning and tea at night.

Visit her online at knockingfrominside.blogspot.com

The Poetry Box Chapbook Prize

In 2018, The Poetry Box® introduced their annual Chapbook Prize competition. The contest is open to both established poets and emerging talent alike, and the editors reserve the right to select more than one poet's manuscript for publication. Currently, the contest is open to poets residing in the United States and is open for submissions each year during the month of February. Find more information at ThePoetryBox.com.

2020 Winners:

The Day of My First Driving Lesson by Tiel Aisha Ansari

My Mother Never Died Before by Marcia B. Loughran

Off Coldwater Canyon by C.W. Emerson

2019 Winners:

Moroccan Holiday by Lauren Tivey

Hello, Darling by Christine Higgins

Falling into the River by Debbie Hall

2018 Winners:

Shrinking Bones by Judy K. Mosher

November Quilt by Penelope Scambly Schott

14: Antología del Sonoran by Christopher Bogart

Fireweed by Gudrun Bortman